"Wiggles," Stomps, and Squeezes Calm My Jitters Down

LINDSEY ROWE PARKER

Illustrated by
REBECCA BURGESS

Published in the United States by BQB Publishing
(an imprint of Boutique of Quality Books Publishing Company)
www.bqbpublishing.com

978-1-945448-92-8 (hc)
978-1-945448-93-5 (e)
978-1-945448-94-2 (audio)
978-1-952782-68-8 (p)

Library of Congress Control Number: 2020946889

Cover and interior illustrations: Rebecca Burgess
Interior Design Setup: Robin Krauss, www.bookformatters.com
Editor: Andrea Berns

Praises for Wiggles, Stomps, and Squeezes

"*Wiggles, Stomps, and Squeezes* playfully validates the unique sensory experiences of children, written from their own perspective. I'm excited for every kid that will see themselves in this beautiful book!"

— Mark Loewen, Author of *What Does a Princess Really Look Like?*

"I often find myself trying to explain to parents why their child needs wiggles, stomps, and squeezes to get through their day while experiencing sensory input in ways that are different and often more intense. This is the first book I have come across that provides a very real glimpse into the lived experience of a child with sensory differences. What a wonderful book that so many families can benefit from!"

— Caitlyn Berry, Occupational Therapist

"I have worked in special education for 12 years and have not come across a book that explains these jittery feelings until now. This book will capture the hearts of families and children with unique needs as well as educate those unfamiliar with sensory differences."

— Bridget Martinez, Special Education Teacher

Dedications

For my kiddos, Thank you for teaching me more about myself every day. We are all enough just as we are.

— Lindsey

———————

For Mum, Thank you for truly letting me be completely me, I grew up to be confident in myself because of you. ✕ ✕ ✕

— Bex

I need a
SQUISH
I need a
SQUEEZE

I can't explain why.

I get jitters down deep inside and it makes me want to run!

2

How fast
can I go?

My feet zing when
they hit the ground.

3

Whap-
Whap-
whap

Round and round I zoom,
touching every wall.

I giggle and shriek,
my voice loud
inside my head.

4

I need to wiggle.
I need to tap!
I can't explain why.

6

The steaming pile
of mush in front of me
smells weird and
looks squishy.

I push the
food away.

But my tummy growls
and my jitters come back.

8

My spoon is heavy in my hand.

TaP-TaP

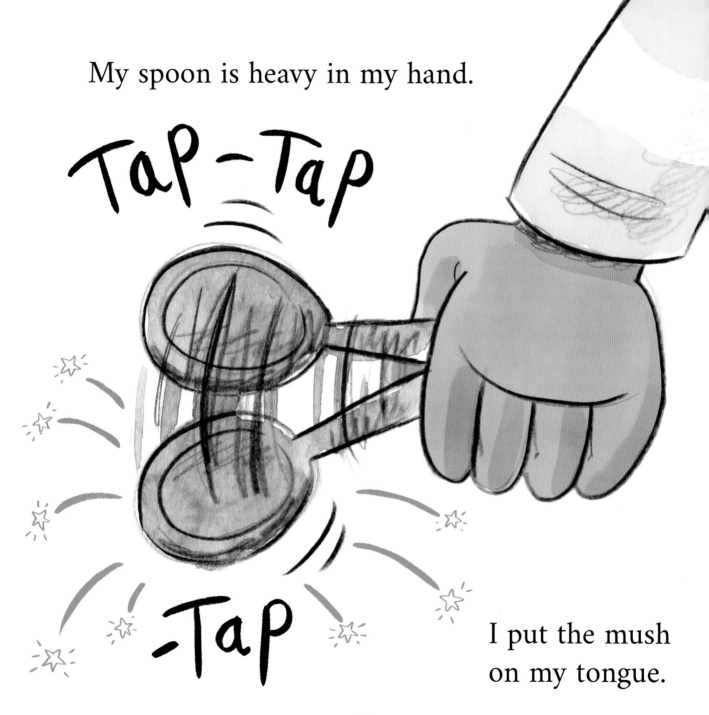

-TaP

I put the mush
on my tongue.

I roll it around,
squish it in
my cheeks,

swish it through
my teeth.

11

That's what calms
my jitters down.

I need to zoom, I need to stomp!
I can't explain why.

My shirt pulls over my head with a

Whoosh

My hair is tickly on my face.

15

Where are my hands?

I can't move! I'm stuck!

Push, Push, Push.

One arm
pops through.

Push, Push, Push.

Two arms
pop through.

17

WAIT!

Now it's time for feet.
I lift my foot as
high as I can.

I check to make sure they are the good pants. No tag.

Are these the itchy pants?

20

OK.
One step, two step.

Hop, hop, hop.

"One more time" mom says.
I need to zoom!

Push, Push,
Push.

Push, Push,
Push.

One shoe goes on.

Two shoes go on.

"Test your shoes."

I smile and stomp, stomp, stomp.
And it calms my jitters down.

I need to swing. I need to fly!
I can't explain why.

The cool air rushes against my face,
through my hair. The strands tickle my cheeks.

My shoes sparkle as they speed toward the sky.
Will I fall? I squint my eyes to see
and the pull of the earth draws me down.

26

Then once again

UP-UP-UP!

And it calms my jitters down.

I need to hum. I need to sway!
I can't explain why.

I grab the sand in my hand
looking at each pebble.

Big pebbles, little pebbles.

Pebbles that crunch and grind
between my fingers.

Tiny specks of sand
cover my hands.

I shake it off. It won't come clean.
I wipe it off again and again.

I wipe my hands down
my shirt, down my pants.

All the way to my shoes.

Yuck. Wipe again.

31

My jitters are getting loud now.
I hum louder.

Maybe if I shake my hands it will go away?

My jitters are roaring in my ears!
Why won't it come off?! I am crying.

Everything is loud.
My tears are loud too.

Mom hugs me. I don't want a hug.
I want the specks off me.

I push away.
Everything is too loud.

Water swirls down the drain.

Swirl, swirl, swirl

My specks start to disappear.
I rub my hands together.

Swish, swish, swish

39

My tears are quieter now. I can finally hear my hum.

Mom hums too.
That's what calms my jitters down.

I need a squish. I need a squeeze!
I can't explain why.

I squeeze her tight. She smells like soap and waffles.

We sway back and forth,
and mom is warm and soft.

Her hair tickles my face when I snuggle in.

Mom hugs so strong,
so long, so safe.
I hear the

thump-thump
-thump

of her heart.

"I love you" she says.

I don't say anything,
but I squeeze a little tighter.

And it calms my
jitters down.

About the Author

Lindsey is a mom at the tail end of toddler-hood, embracing the next phase of parenting while learning to navigate and advocate for her young autistic daughter. With a recent adult diagnosis of ADHD, and a new deeper understanding of her own sensory experiences, she has begun to delve into the neurodiversity community learning all she can from neurodiverse voices. This is her first picture book, and she hopes it connects with everyone who has felt the need for a wiggle, stomp, or squeeze.

About the Illustrator

Rebecca (Bex) is an autistic illustrator living in the UK. They love history and nature, but comics and illustration most of all! Their passion has led them to work with the likes of The Guardian and Jessica Kingsley Publishing. Bex is most famous for their online comic *Understanding the Spectrum*, a comic explaining autism that has been shared in several books and used by parents, teachers, and doctors.